AF390582

Ruby Quartz

poems about love, and other ways to spell grief.

Vermanda

BookLeaf Publishing

India | USA | UK

Copyright © Vermanda
All Rights Reserved.

This book has been self-published with all reasonable efforts taken to make the material error-free by the author. No part of this book shall be used, reproduced in any manner whatsoever without written permission from the author, except in the case of brief quotations embodied in critical articles and reviews.

The Author of this book is solely responsible and liable for its content including but not limited to the views, representations, descriptions, statements, information, opinions, and references ["Content"]. The Content of this book shall not constitute or be construed or deemed to reflect the opinion or expression of the Publisher or Editor. Neither the Publisher nor Editor endorse or approve the Content of this book or guarantee the reliability, accuracy, or completeness of the Content published herein and do not make any representations or warranties of any kind, express or implied, including but not limited to the implied warranties of merchantability, fitness for a particular purpose.

The Publisher and Editor shall not be liable whatsoever...

Made with ❤ on the BookLeaf Publishing Platform
www.bookleafpub.in
www.bookleafpub.com

Dedication

In memory of my grandfather, the purest form of love i've ever known.

Preface

As you explore this collection, I hope you feel seen in your own experiences, find peace in your moments of solitude, and inspiration in the way love seems to reframe and replenish everything it touches. Whether you are with the love your life, navigating the quiet pain of longing or learning to redefine what love means as you grow, may these words offer you a space to feel, reflect, and maybe even rediscover the many faces of love that guide us. Enter a journey through the heart, a journey that, I hope, will you read and truly feel.

Acknowledgements

I would like to extend my heartfelt gratitude to my
family,
a village built on the practice of love.

Do You See Me?

My eyes beyond weary,
waterfalls fed by oceans.

I'm holding tight to sanity,
with blistered hands,
my grip is slipping.

I screamed help into the ether,
only an echo in return.

Where are you now,
my constant guide in the dark?

Adjust the sun,
I need your warmth.

Arrange the stars,
spell out you love me.

Breathe into the wind,
remind me again,
it's ok.

In my head it's always raining,
spread the clouds,
Then just maybe you could see me.

In The Morning

Leave the flour on the floor,
I'll mop it another time.
Press your lips to mine some more,
I'll pour us some wine.

Forget the dishes in the sink,
They need to soak anyway.
I don't want room to think,
Just kiss my breath away.

I know the kitchen is a mess,
just appreciate our sweet bonding,
take my hands and trace your chest,
I'll clean it in the morning.

Diamond

I release you with this burning twine,
a disconnect long overdue.

I erase your promises from my mind,
which, like everything else,
fell through.

I instead replace your decite,
with my undeniable truth.

I loved you in my purest form,
our failure falls upon you.

I loved you at your darkest times,
some months the sun didn't rise.

I stayed, drunk on loyalty,
even with all your sobering lies.

I pour this mana back into my worth,
no longer burdened by your baggage.

I pick myself up from the dirt,
a diamond too enduring to truly damage.

Coming Undone

A little white thread,
curiosity gave a tug,
my eyes darkened,
face fell,
shoulders dropped,
heart broke,
stomach sank,
knees weakened,
irrevocably and definitively torn,
Intertwined with your cut of cloth,
makes sense I'd unravel.

Oceans Apart

You bought flowers, quickly wilting,
petals drying and dying,
like our bond.

We shared awkward showers,
steam mingling with tension,
stale arguements nobody won.

You gave shallow thoughtless gifts,
trying to fill deep wounds.
Still,
all material things must break,
and so would we soon.

Since I can't forget her,
you learned to despise me.
Silence stretched over days,
forming an abyss in my heart;
if you don't hold me tighter,
I'll drift away.

I built a boat of hollowed promises,
pitched my pride to set sail,

floating slowly past our memories,
I blew a kiss and bid you well.

DÉJÀ VU

This passion like possession,
secrets woven through my DNA,
Are you a dream made real?
Somehow, we met before today.

Did our paths cross in a past life?
Stars of the same constellation?
Dark matter from the same place,
in space?
Why is there no hesitation?

Your eyes speak a silent language,
one I didn't know I knew, to forget.

Did we meet on Pangea, before the land split?
You awaken some dormant part of me,
rising swiftly like a tide.

Your smile, so intimately familiar,
we must have been lovers from a lost tribe,
with so much unspoken history.

How do I simply say, Hi?

Surrender

Im begging you,
please go right now,
I don't know how to leave,
loneliness,
my consistent friend,
abandonment,
like family.

I find frustration in confrontation,
too passive,
no aggression,
now that everything has fallen apart,
you'd think I'd learn my lesson.

Still I can't breathe to speak to you,
my heart ahead of my mind,
you raise your voice,
hoping now you could reach me,
but I *need* galaxies,
I *need* time.

Letting go is bittersweet,
freedom is seldom well dressed,
yes, I know,

I was broken before,
but for you?
I fought to give my best.

Memories unmoved by time,
replaying, somehow off cue,
I prayed they'd fade between the years,
intimate scenes,
tainted by betrayal,
and stained blue.

Traces of my soul run deep,
they still shape and guide your steps,
our love lost in your intricacies,
your devotion forever lacking depth.

After having complete control of me,
I gave,
you took,
until there was
nothing left.

What more can I surrender?

To Die For

For this precious little time?
yet even that is borrowed.

The faint fragile faith I hold?
then how will I face the dawn tommorow?

What then could I offer,
so elusive is your affection.

My endless wishful dreams?
a constant yearning for connection.

If I break my neck,
to end your thirst,
let you drink me dry.

Tell me, is this the price of love?

All I'd have to do for you then,
is die.

Me, Myself, and I

A heart you didn't break is still broken,
words hurt more left unspoken.

Anxiety isn't a pass,
but a diagnosis.

Your words are loaded,
Aimed at my vulnerablity.

Speak.

Im blown away,
bleeding out, screaming out,

Love me anyway.

I know I'm imperfect,
pleading: I'm still worth it.

Growing pains between us,
praying you still need us.

Take me with you if you're leaving,
I don't want my momma grieving.

The last time I was left with me,
was an odyssey ending in therapy.
I did my best to get shards out of dust.

Pressure is supposed to make diamonds,
yet, im obsessive, compulsive,
just decorative names for my many faces.

With me and myself at constant war,
how can I ask anyone to pay in peace?

Experimental

Let's embrace this without trying,
we don't have to define divinity,
love is far from a perfect science.

Like the weight of the intangible name,
so dense in its abilities,
it can **transform a flicker into a flame.**

Not everything can be explained.

Miracles don't ask to be perceived,
yet I close my eyes, there you are,
strikingly vivid in my dreams.

Wisdom flirts with insanity,
to be aware yet still so intrigued.
All past experiments have failed,
If you are just a man,
how is this any different?
Why do you mean everything to me?

Numb Noise

Waterproof mascara is a myth.

If pews could speak,
they'd tell of trembling legs,
soulful prayers, and
the looped cacophony of never-ending hurt.

How at times,
even they can't bear the weight,
of overwhelming sorrow.

The choir sweetly sang,
His eye is on the sparrow,
I know he watches me,
but not even Lauryn with all her hills of hope,
could eclipse deep suffering.

Every praying hand held together,
still can't fill the void.

In your wake, you leave no shame,
only a tiny girl who grins like you.

Life prepares trees for the burial of seeds,

but it left us to grieve.

Yet the preacher says, 'Let your will be done'.
now here's Mother Nature, hiding away her son.

Rapid thoughts clouded by fleeting noise;
In silence, a struggle to find calm.

A beautiful, blessed homegoing,
leaving hearts so vacant,
no room for any emotion,
The only feeling now is numb.

Suffocate

Winds are invisible,
whether they carry leaves or change,
forces faint to our sight,
only left with wreckage after it rains.

The only proof we ever existed,
a hollow home, reduced to its bones,
littered with shattered frames,
housing poorly painted pictures.
scraps of snapped walls,
split foundations and decisions.

You found safety in my heart's shelter,
rebuilding with you until times got better,
Alone, crafting an atmosphere for growth.

Still you say I am your reason to breathe

For you, air was always there,
Never mind how I'm polluted,
I take my oxygen and dissipate-
suffocate.

You didn't have to cheat,
you knew you could always leave.

18

Love Letter

You were a child,
still so young,
now filled with confusion and regret,
you didn't believe,
monsters are real,
now you'll never forget,

That was real,
not a dream,
you pretended to be asleep,
suddenly you were suffocating,
under nothing but your sheets,
the fabric grew heavy,
you couldn't move,
it held down your hands and feet.

A burst of tears,
the spell was broken,
you escaped to a safe space,
choking, shaking,
standing in the mirror,
you didn't recognize your face.

Your eyes were dull,

two empty voids,
windows to a vacant home,
your innocence, a distant thought,
you felt all your worth was gone.

You held a blade,
pressed into your neck,
It was blunt and you were eight,
your small hands, shaking, dragging,
scared,
you didn't have the strength.

No merciful release of death,
You would draw a different pain,
along with this new sense of fear,
your fresh scars screamed shame.

I tried yelling,
I still love you!
but I know you couldn't hear,
too far to ever trust yourself,
too many voices in your ear,
crowding in your head,

I don't care, what grandma said,
you are not your absent father
brilliant, couragous, and graceful,

you are nothing like that coward.

Built altogether wonderful,
yes I know what went through,
I was there,
I'm still here,
You only ever needed you.

Direct Quote

Seat belts hold you in place,
no matter how hard you're crashing.

My dignity was totaled,
maybe If I had worn mines,
it would've only been dented,

Still parked,
cruising through conversation,
I suddenly became aware,
my chest tightened,
as my pulse quickened,
Is this memory lane?
Why are we here?

I can't remember,
which you locked first,
was it the doors,
my arms or knees?

Constraining me didn't hurt,
not as much as being decieved,
I trusted you,
shared the pain of my past,

how could you still do this to me?

"you love me, so you didn't mean no."

Familiar

Whenever my mind felt foreign,
I'd pack my baggage,
and go home—
The only place I've never felt alone,
Ironically, now sits empty,
even though inside,
I still see you sitting,
drinking coffee.

Don't You Miss Dancing?

Remember,
a tornado of talent,
gracefully tearing through stages,
transcending standards,
challenging society's expectations.

Tenacity in every turn,
sophisticated in every spin,
determined in every drop,
you had undivided attention then.

Colors within your rhythm,
inspiring crowds to their feet,
joy in your footwork,
I know you miss dancing,
a love that set you free.

Crown

You wore resilience like a crown,
no paths paved with gold,
no silver spoons,
or helping hands.
only you,
alone.

Through late nights, and early mornings,
you would trade your comfort for mine,
taking every chance, at whatever job,
all so we could shine.

Everyday, all at once, you were a coach,
cook, and maid, all just after work,
overtime unpaid.

Currency expressed through gratitude,
you raised us, while still growing up.
a choice beyond sacrifice,
I could only call love.

My Sisters Keeper

When God made my sister,
He knew I'd need a friend,
A safe space, to be myself,
A bond that will not end.

When God gave me my sister,
No words could ever explain,
I vowed to keep her
from that moment,
shielding her from pain.

Thank you God, for my sister,
I'm grateful to watch her grow
teaching her to trust herself,
and let her light glow.

Please, God protect my sister.
she's grown beyond my arms,
never far out of my reach,
yet I cant keep her safe from harm.

She's going places, achieving goals,
reaching higher heights

keep her eyes wide, feet grounded,
and her worth centered in sight.

Questions

If lightning rarely strikes twice,
how can I, three times,
be a victim?
How many please no's, and
let me go's,
before my body is only mine?
or, Is this,
love?

Dear Daniel

I got a tattoo to
immortalize my grief.
I know my body
won't last forever,
but till then,
you're etched in me.

You deserve a symbol of life;
yours was far too short.
I still can't make sense of that day—
in a flash, our world fell apart.

A rift so swift, so violent, and finite;
whenever I think of you in that room,
I can't sleep for a few nights.

You held my heart for less than a year,
and for over a decade, I've wept.
I told myself you were asleep then,
and ever since, in my heart, you have slept.

Desert Flower

a lone cactus, in my depleted desert,
vicariously you grew,
Anything living here before,
had long since whitered.

In your shadow, I found solace,
A bond budding, steadily blooming
You, a seed of persistence,
In my heart, you took root.

Your flowers, bright against the sand,
Coloring the gray of my days,
A reminder that life can flourish,
Even in the toughest ways.

To embrace the storms, the drought,
the pain, after all that, came you,
my son, destined, against the dark,
you shone through.

www.ingramcontent.com/pod-product-compliance
Lightning Source LLC
LaVergne TN
LVHW010835200726
843508LV00012B/2613

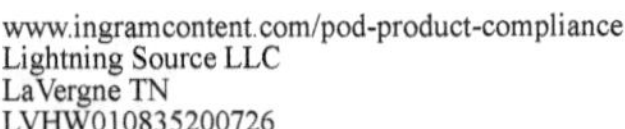